GHOSTS

Aaron Frisch

CREATIVE EDUCATION

Published by Creative Education
P.O. Box 227, Mankato, Minnesota 56002
Creative Education is an imprint of
The Creative Company
www.thecreativecompany.us

Design and production by
Christine Vanderbeek
Art direction by **Rita Marshall**
Printed in the United States of America

Photographs by Alamy (GARY DOAK,
Photos 12, Marc Tielemans), Dreamstime
(Sandra Cunningham, Reinhold Leitner),
Getty Images (John Gollop, M. Eric
Honeycutt, Jacobs Stock Photography,
Maria Pavlova, Todd Warnock),
iStockphoto (Plus), Shutterstock
(Mikhail), Veer (James Griehaber,
Richard Kegler), Wikipedia (John Leech)

**Library of Congress
Cataloging-in-Publication Data**
Frisch, Aaron.
Ghosts / Aaron Frisch.
p. cm. — (That's spooky!)
Summary: A basic but fun exploration of
ghosts—spirits known for their haunting
behavior—including how they come to
exist, their weaknesses, and memorable
examples from pop culture.
Includes bibliographical references and
index.
ISBN 978-1-60818-246-6
1. Ghosts—Juvenile literature. I. Title.

BF1461.F75 2013
133.1—dc23   2011051178

First edition
9 8 7 6 5 4 3 2 1

CONTENTS

IMAGINE ...

You are spending the night in an old house. You feel cool air on the back of your neck. Then you see a creaky door move. Suddenly, a white shape floats through the wall!

IT'S A GHOST!

WHAT IS A GHOST?

A ghost is the spirit of a dead person. A ghost might look like mist or be **INVISIBLE**. Sometimes a ghost inhabits an object. This means it goes inside the object and uses it like a body.

Some ghosts like to hang out around graveyards

BECOMING A GHOST

Ghosts are formed when people die but leave something in their lives unfinished. Some ghosts want to get **REVENGE**. Other people become ghosts because they did something bad when they were alive.

Many ghosts seem to be sad or lonely

GHOST BEHAVIOR

A ghost usually **HAUNTS** a certain place. It might make spooky sounds or move things around to scare people away. If a ghost finishes a certain task, it might get to rest and not be a ghost anymore.

It can be hard to sleep with a ghost around

A Ghost's Powers

A ghost can go almost anywhere. It can float through walls or floors. People cannot touch most ghosts. A ghost's main power is being just plain spooky. A really scary ghost can make people **FAINT**!

Ghosts can pass through brick walls or glass

A Ghost's Weaknesses

Most ghosts cannot touch living people. They can only do things to scare them. Some people think that salt keeps ghosts away. Noisy bells can be used to chase away a ghost, too.

A bell might keep a ghost out of your house

15

FAMOUS GHOSTS

There are many movies about ghosts. In *Ghostbusters*, four men catch all kinds of ghosts. One of the ghosts is called Slimer. It is a green ghost that floats around and eats as much food as it can.

Slimer (left) and the Ghostbusters (right)

16

Sometimes ghosts are helpful. In the story *A Christmas Carol*, three ghosts try to help a **GREEDY** man be a better person. Casper is a cartoon ghost that gets tired of scaring people and tries to make friends instead.

Casper (left); a *Christmas Carol* ghost (above)

DO SOME HAUNTING

Ghosts are not real. They are only parts of stories and movies. But acting like a ghost can be fun. Put a white sheet over your head. (Make sure you can see through it.) Then try to give your family or friends the goosebumps!

A sheet is the quick way to become a ghost

LEARN TO SPOT A GHOST

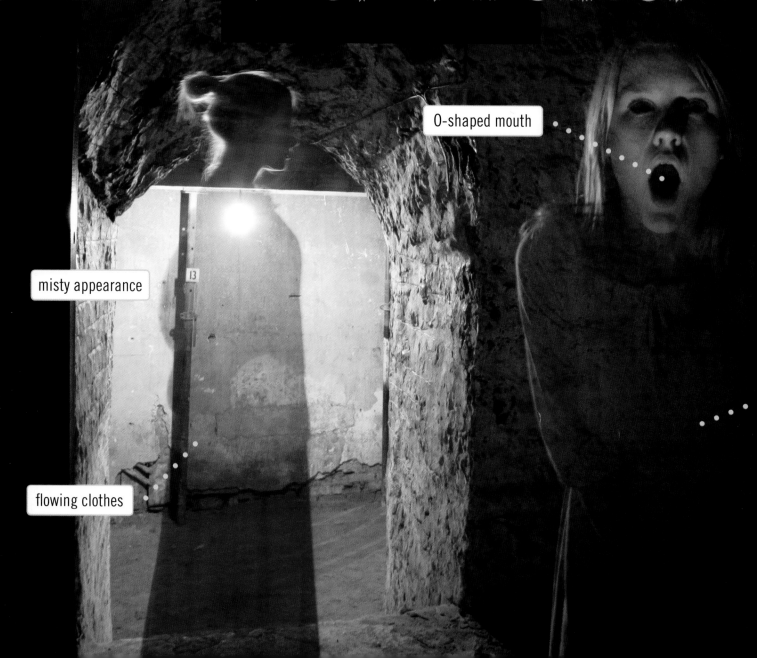

O-shaped mouth

misty appearance

flowing clothes

THAT'S SPOOKY!

DICTIONARY

floating "body"

FAINT pass out or go to sleep very suddenly

GREEDY wanting to make or keep a lot of money all for yourself

HAUNTS visits a place a lot, usually in a spooky way

INVISIBLE unable to be seen

REVENGE do something bad to people because they did something bad to you

THAT'S SPOOKY!

GHOSTS

READ MORE

Hamilton, S. L. *Ghosts*. Edina, Minn.: Abdo, 2011.

Pipe, Jim. *Ghosts*. New York: Bearport, 2007.

Schwartz, Alvin. *Ghosts!: Ghostly Tales from Folklore*.
    New York: HarperCollins, 1991.

WEB SITES

DISCOVERY KIDS: ZAP A GHOST

http://kids.discovery.com/games/skill/zap-a-ghost

This site has a video game with ghosts in a spooky old house.

FUNSCHOOL: HALLOWEEN

http://funschool.kaboose.com/fun-blaster/halloween/

This site has a lot of spooky games and pictures for coloring.

INDEX